THE M·O·V·I·E·S

OF ALFRED HITCHCOCK

THE ·M·O·V·I·E·S
OF ALFRED HITCHCOCK

by Judy Arginteanu

Lerner Publications Company
Minneapolis

Page two: Alfred Hitchcock and Anthony Perkins take a break from the filming of *Psycho*.

Acknowledgments

The photographs in this book are reproduced through the courtesy of: pp. 1, 30, 34, 47, 51, 52, 61, 75, Cleveland Public Library; pp. 2, 6, 15, 27, 49, 64, 69, 76, 78, Hollywood Book and Poster; pp. 9, 38, 43, 56, 65, Wisconsin Center for Film and Theatre Research; pp. 11, 16, Collectors Bookstore; pp. 12, 22, Museum of Modern Art Film Stills Archive; pp. 17, 20, 21, 24, 25, 28, 33, 37, 40, 41, 45, 54, 55, 58, 62, 72, 73, Cinema Collectors; p. 67, Moving Image and Sound Archives, Public Archives of Canada.

Front cover photograph courtesy of Hollywood Book and Poster.
Back cover photograph courtesy of Moving Image and Sound Archives, Public Archives of Canada.

LIBRARY OF CONGRESS CATALOGING-IN-PUBLICATION DATA

Arginteanu, Judy
   The movies of Alfred Hitchcock / by Judy Arginteanu.
     p. cm.
   Includes bibliographical references and index.
   Summary: Analyzes the ideas and themes of the famous film director and discusses individual movies including "Vertigo," "Psycho," and "The Birds."
   ISBN 0-8225-1642-X
   1. Hitchcock, Alfred, 1899- —Criticism and interpretation—Juvenile literature. [1. Hitchcock, Alfred, 1899- —Criticism and interpretation. 2. Motion pictures—History and criticism.]
I. Title.
PN1998.3.H58A74 1994
791.43'0233'092—dc20   93-23990
                                            CIP
                                            AC

Manufactured in the United States of America
1 2 3 4 5 6 -I/JR- 99 98 97 96 95 94

Contents

Introduction

Alfred Hitchcock—the name itself means "suspense." Even if you have never seen one of his movies, you probably know that they are delightfully thrilling and scary.

For over 40 years, Hitchcock kept movie audiences on the edge of their seats. Scenes from his films have become an enduring part of American popular culture: the crop-duster plane chasing Cary Grant in *North by Northwest,* the carousel in *Strangers on a Train,* and the famous shower scene from *Psycho* (a scene that made a lot of people decide to take baths for a few years!).

With his trademark walk-on parts in his own movies, and as host of the "Alfred Hitchcock Presents" TV show in the late 1950s and early 1960s, Hitchcock was one of the few directors whose face the public recognized. He played an important role in getting the public to care about who directed a movie as well as which actors starred in it. By the end of his life, Hitchcock's name often received top billing on movie theater marquees, above the names of famous actors.

The "master of suspense," as he came to be known, was born in 1899 outside London. A shy boy who kept to himself, he had a rather ordinary childhood, but one incident that occurred when he was five years old left quite an impression. His father had sent him to the police station with a note. When Hitchcock got there, the police officers followed the instructions on the note—which told them to lock the boy up for being naughty! Hitchcock said the brief jailing cemented his lifelong fear of police.

After completing his education in Catholic schools, Hitchcock worked as a technical clerk at a company that manufactured electric cable. When he was in his late teens, he got a job as a layout artist designing advertisements for a department store. With this experience, in 1920 he landed a job as a title artist for movies, writing and designing the words that appeared on-screen at silent movies (sound movies hadn't been invented yet). He moved on to become a screenwriter, assistant director, and production manager. In 1926 he married Alma Reville, an assistant director. The couple worked together on his films throughout his career.

Early in his career, Hitchcock worked for a German film studio, where he soaked up the influence of Expressionism, the prevailing film style in the 1920s. German Expressionism emphasized disturbing themes such as madness and used very dramatic, shadowy lighting. (Two famous German Expressionist movies are *Nosferatu*, one of the first vampire movies, and *The Cabinet of Dr. Caligari*, about an evil scientist.)

Hitchcock directed his first movie, *The Pleasure Garden*, in 1925 and his first thriller, *The Lodger*, a year later (both were silent movies). He made the first British sound film, *Blackmail*, in 1929. By the mid-1930s, the director was

Producer David Selznick and Hitchcock worked together on *Rebecca* and other films.

well established, with such successful films as *The Man Who Knew Too Much* (which he remade in 1956), *The 39 Steps*, and *The Lady Vanishes*.

In 1939 Hitchcock moved to Hollywood, California, and signed a contract with movie mogul David O. Selznick, whose studio had just produced the blockbuster *Gone With the Wind*. Hitchcock's first American movie, *Rebecca*, won an Academy Award for best picture in 1940, and Hitchcock was nominated for best director.

Hitchcock made 13 more movies in the 1940s, including *Spellbound,* with Ingrid Bergman as a psychiatrist, Gregory Peck as her patient, and a dream sequence with sets designed by the surrealist artist Salvador Dali. The following decade, 1950 to 1960, was what some critics consider

Hitchcock's golden period, when he made a string of great movies: *Strangers on a Train, Rear Window, To Catch a Thief, The Trouble with Harry, Vertigo, North by Northwest,* and *Psycho.* In 1955 "Alfred Hitchcock Presents" made its television debut.

Hitchcock—or "Hitch," as he was nicknamed—continued to produce moneymaking films during the 1960s and early 1970s, although critics did not always like the movies of those years. Hitchcock's final movie was *Family Plot,* released in 1976. The director died in 1980.

Despite his success, Hitchcock the shy boy grew into Hitchcock the shy man. He was so modest that people sometimes wondered how such a quiet, well-mannered, "normal" man could make movies as horrifying as *Psycho* and *The Birds.* But, while those movies are scary, they draw their power more from suspense than from horror.

Hitchcock had very clear ideas about suspense. Suspense is not the same as surprise. A suspense movie is not a "whodunit" detective mystery, and certainly not a "slasher" movie, even though these kinds of films might use suspense from time to time.

According to Hitchcock, suspense happens when the audience knows something the characters in the movie don't know. He explained the difference between suspense and surprise like this: Suppose you see a group of people sitting around a table, making small talk. Suddenly a bomb goes off. That's shocking, but the scene will only keep you on the edge of your seat if you know the bomb is hidden under the table. Then, as the characters chatter away, you want to shout, "Get out of there, a bomb is about to go off!" The fact that the people are talking about something trivial heightens the suspense. But,

Hitchcock said, if you create suspense, "you must also relieve it." The bomb must not be allowed to go off.

Hitchcock avoided predictable situations. In *North By Northwest*, Cary Grant is sent to a mysterious place, and the audience knows that his life is probably in danger. But instead of the usual dark, sinister alley, Grant is sent to a midwestern road in broad daylight—about as ordinary, unthreatening a place as you could think of. It's only when a bystander notices that there is a crop-duster airplane— but no crops—do we realize that Grant is in danger.

A famous scene from *North by Northwest*

Hitchcock also used a trick he called a "MacGuffin" to heighten suspense. A MacGuffin, according to Hitchcock, is something in the plot of a movie that seems very important to the characters but, in the end, turns out to have little impact. In *The 39 Steps,* for example, the secret the spies are trying to steal is a bunch of garbled equations; it really doesn't matter what the equations mean, but the pursuit of those secrets sends the characters all over the Scottish moors and back to London.

Not only did Hitchcock have a definite idea of what suspense was, but he was a master at using the special tools of filmmaking to add to the suspense. Hitchcock carefully planned out an entire movie in advance. He first sketched out every shot on a "storyboard" (sort of like a comic book version of the movie). And whenever possible, he chose

Alfred Hitchcock, his wife Alma Reville, and their daughter Patricia

to *show* rather than tell. He liked to build a scene from many shots by emphasizing one detail, then another, drawing the audience into the situation.

Building up a movie from many shots is called editing (also known as "montage" or "cutting," because the individual pieces of film are actually cut up and put together in different sequences). A very famous example of Hitchcock's fast cutting or editing is the shower scene in *Psycho*. He spent 7 days assembling the 78 cuts (78 different pieces of film) for a total of 45 seconds on-screen.

Although Hitchcock is now recognized as a special talent, for many years, critics dismissed his movies as no more than popular entertainment for the public. Just because his movies were entertaining, however, doesn't mean he didn't bring up important ideas. He just did it more sneakily than a lot of "serious" movie directors. Hitchcock said it was easy to make an "artistic" film—the trick was to make a film that would sell a lot of tickets!

In the 1950s, a group of French movie critics (most of whom went on to become well-known directors themselves) began to write about Hitchcock as a serious artist. They considered him an *auteur* (the French word for "author"). Because it takes a crew of many people to make a movie, the director's influence on the final product is often limited. A film "auteur," however, leaves his or her own special, recognizable imprint on a movie, just like an author who writes a book that reflects a personal sensibility or way of seeing life.

Part of the fun of a Hitchcock movie is experiencing the same anxiety that the characters feel in a world that seems to be losing all rhyme or reason. Hitchcock creates suspense by exploring disturbing ideas, particularly about the way good and evil are sometimes interlocked.

Often in Hitchcock movies, a good person and a bad person swap identities. The good person does things he or she wouldn't normally do, or sympathizes with the bad person. In *Shadow of a Doubt,* for example, the two main characters have the same name—the niece is nicknamed "Charlie" after her favorite (and, as it turns out, evil) uncle.

Hitchcock's villains are often attractive, intelligent, even charming. Danger is scarier if it happens on our own street, in broad daylight, among people like the people we know. Then we must face our fears.

Hitchcock's view of romance was also slightly twisted. Although he himself led a very quiet family life, his movie couples always seem to be battling in some way. But their fights add an edge to their romance. Mixing romance, mystery, and murder made for a thrilling combination. Hitchcock liked to quote the English writer Oscar Wilde: "Each man kills the thing he loves."

Hitchcock's leading ladies also seem to follow a pattern. He preferred standoffish blonds, including Madeleine Carroll in *The 39 Steps*; Grace Kelly (who starred in three Hitchcock movies); Kim Novak, who played both a blond and a brunet in *Vertigo*; Eva Marie Saint (*North by Northwest*); Janet Leigh in *Psycho*; and Tippi Hedren (*The Birds, Marnie*). What's more, he seemed to enjoy pushing these women off their pedestals.

Compared to contemporary slasher movies, Hitchcock's movies are not very violent. He decided to shoot *Psycho* in black-and-white film because he worried that audiences would be shocked to see so much blood in color. Nevertheless, he was criticized because his movies always involved murder. Hitchcock defended himself by saying that his movies were no more violent than Hansel and Gretel pushing an old woman into an oven.

Hitchcock and Janet Leigh share a laugh on the set of *Psycho*. The director was sometimes mean to his leading ladies.

Still, the director did like to joke about death in a way that some people didn't consider proper. Asked what kind of murder he'd choose for himself, he replied calmly, "Well, there are many nice ways: Eating is a good one." In discussing the plot of a movie with a writer one day, Hitchcock referred to "that lovely moment when we say, 'Wouldn't it be fun to kill him this way?'"

Note: the following abbreviations are used in this book:
 b/w black and white
 pro producer
 sc screenplay by
 st starring

(1935)
THE 39 STEPS

b/w

pro Michael Balcon, Ivor Montagu
sc Charles Bennett and Alma Reville, from the novel by John Buchan
st Madeleine Carroll (Pamela), Robert Donat (Richard Hannay), Lucie Mannheim (Miss Smith), Peggy Ashcroft (farmer's wife)

The *39 Steps*, Hitchcock's first major feature film, was a big hit in Britain and the United States and established his reputation as an international director. It was also one of Hitchcock's favorite movies. He liked the way the hero (Robert Donat) jumped from one outlandish situation to another, with little transition.

The movie contains most of the major themes that Hitchcock goes on to refine later. It has a basic mystery plot, in which an accidental event sets off the action. An innocent man, presumed guilty by the authorities, is caught in a web of intrigue that he doesn't clearly understand, and he must assume a different identity to protect his true (guiltless) self. Characters are not what they seem, including an upstanding citizen who is actually a villain. The movie has a light, sophisticated, comic tone, especially in the verbal sparring between the two romantic leads. It also has the stock Hitchcock characters and situations: an icy blond woman; a journey; and a MacGuffin. And, of course, the audience knows more than the characters, a crucial factor for suspense.

"What Are the 39 Steps?"

Richard Hannay is a young Canadian visiting England. Among the attractions at a music hall variety show Hannay attends is trivia expert Mr. Memory, who remembers and recites facts with complete accuracy.

The show is disrupted by gunshots, and in the commotion a strange woman with a foreign accent accosts Hannay, asking for protection. Back at his flat, "Miss Smith" reveals she is a foreign-born spy working for England. (In this scene especially, we can see the influence of the German Expressionist style of filmmaking in the moody use of light and shadow.) She fired the shots herself to create a diversion so that she wouldn't be killed. She says she is on the trail of "the 39 steps," but she doesn't explain what they are. She must go to Scotland to track down the man who turns out to be the villain. This man, she tells Hannay, is missing part of his pinky.

Before she can leave, however, she is murdered—and Hannay is the prime suspect. He is also pursued by some mysterious bad guys, who know he has learned something about "Miss Smith's" mission. To escape, he flees in a milkman's uniform.

The police tail Hannay throughout his train journey to Scotland. Even though he's innocent, he worries about being caught. In the train, he tries to escape notice by kissing a strange woman, but she refuses to pretend she knows him and gives him away to the police. Still, he manages to elude the police and hides on a railway bridge.

In the Scottish highlands, he searches for the town Miss Smith spoke of. An old farmer and his young, unhappy wife take him in for the night. The farmer is suspicious when he sees his wife and Hannay exchange glances—he suspects adultery. This scene is an excellent example of how Hitchcock uses "silent" filming—he shows everything through the action, with few words of dialogue.

The wife helps Hannay escape across the moors, with the police after him. He finds shelter in a mansion, where the maid covers for him without blinking an eye. The master of the house, "the professor," is having a birthday party for his daughter and invites "Mr. Hammond," as Hannay calls himself, to attend. The local sheriff discusses the whereabouts of the murderer, whose escape has made news all over Britain.

The professor calls Mr. Hammond in for a chat and Hannay tells him Miss Smith's story, including the part about the missing finger. The man holds up his hand— part of his pinky is missing! He sets up Hannay's murder to look like a suicide and calmly shoots him.

But Hannay has been spared. When he left the farm, he took the old farmer's coat; the hymnbook in the breast pocket blocked the bullet. As he tells his story to the local sheriff, the sheriff says he's never seen anything like it "except in the movies."

Once more, however, people are not what they seem. The sheriff only pretended to believe Hannay. He turns him over to Scotland Yard, the famous British detective force. Hannay breaks out of the police station window and assumes a series of false identities. First he joins a parade of marchers. Then he accidentally slips into a political meeting, where he's introduced as the featured speaker. He makes a speech that expresses vague political sentiments, as well as his own predicament.

Pamela, the woman Hannay kissed on the train, leads the police to him and they hustle him out of the meeting. Unfortunately, they don't take him to the station—the "police" work for the professor. Instead, the men handcuff Hannay and Pamela together. The two escape through the thick fog on the moors. She refuses to believe the truth and will only cooperate with Hannay after he scares her by saying he is a vicious murderer.

At the hall where Hannay gave a speech, Pamela turns him over to the police.

Hannay and Pamela are stuck together.

Hitchcock viewed the handcuffed pair as "an unhappy married couple." He also got a little kick out of having Madeleine Carroll, a big star at the time, dragged around looking wet, dirty, and ridiculous.

At an inn, Pamela and Hannay pretend to be a married couple, taking a room with a single bed, to Pamela's dismay. Hannay continues to whistle a tune that keeps running through his head.

Later, Pamela awakes and squeezes out of the handcuff. As she prepares to flee, she overhears the professor's men questioning the innkeeper. (The innkeeper's wife covers for them; even though she suspects they're unmarried, she's on the side of young lovers.) Finally convinced that Hannay's spy story is true, Pamela returns to the room and travels to London with Hannay.

In London, Scotland Yard confirms there is a government secret. When Pamela won't reveal Hannay's whereabouts, the police follow her. Hannay is now doubly trapped, fleeing both cops and criminals.

Pamela meets him at the same music hall where the movie began. The professor is also there to link up with another spy. Hannay identifies the professor by his missing pinky. He also identifies that tune he's been whistling.

The final scene takes place back at the music hall.

He heard it the last time he was at the hall, when he saw Mr. Memory—who is part of the spy ring and has memorized the secret.

The police grab Hannay, dismissing his story about Mr. Memory. As Hannay is being dragged off, he screams out, "What are the 39 steps?" Mr. Memory answers, "The 39 steps is an organization of spies collecting information on behalf of...." He falls, shot by the professor.

The professor is collared by the police and hustled off to jail. In the wings, Mr. Memory lays dying as the chorus girls kick up their heels in the background. He recites the secret—a complicated equation—and heaves a sigh of relief, glad to have it off his mind. Then he dies.

THE MACGUFFIN

The 39 Steps features a prominent MacGuffin. A MacGuffin, Hitchcock said, is "something the characters... care a lot about, but the audience doesn't worry about too much." In *The 39 Steps*, the MacGuffin is the secret that the spies are willing to kill for. But when Mr. Memory finally recites the secret at the end, it's just a lot of complicated gibberish that no one really understands. It makes no difference at all to our enjoyment of the movie.

According to Hitchcock, the word *MacGuffin* comes from a story about two men traveling on a train in England. One man says to the other, "What's in that package in the baggage rack above your head?"

"Oh, that's a MacGuffin," replies his friend.

"What's that?"

"It's used for trapping lions in the Scottish highlands."

"But," says the first man, "there are no lions in the Scottish highlands."

"Then that's no MacGuffin!" answers his friend.

THE LADY VANISHES

b/w
pro Edward Black
sc Sidney Gilliatt and Frank Launder, from
 the novel *The Wheel Spins* by Ethel
 Lina White
st Margaret Lockwood (Iris Henderson),
 Michael Redgrave (Gilbert), Dame May
 Whitty (Miss Froy)

The *Lady Vanishes* represents Hitchcock at the top of his form during his British period. Like *The 39 Steps*, *The Lady Vanishes* is classic British Hitchcock: light, suspenseful, fast paced. The director cast two well-known stars, Margaret Lockwood and Dame May Whitty, in leading roles. The part of the male romantic lead went to a young actor in his first starring role, Michael Redgrave. Redgrave is the head of a respected family of British actors, including daughters Lynn and Vanessa Redgrave and granddaughter Natasha Richardson.

The Lady Vanishes was well received in the United States, winning the New York Film Critics Circle awards for best picture and for best director of 1938. It was one of the successes that helped Hitchcock land a contract in Hollywood.

One reason Hitchcock moved to Hollywood was that the studios there would give him more money to make his films. *The Lady Vanishes* was filmed using only one 90-foot-long soundstage. Ironically, the quality that made his British movies so appealing—a distinctly British tension between drama and comedy—gradually disappeared from his American films. Audiences in the U.S. did not seem to understand how such different moods could comfortably exist in the same movie. Hitchcock's American movies took on a darker, scarier tone.

"May Our Enemies...Be Unconscious of Our Purpose."

In an unnamed Alpine country, an avalanche has thrown together an unlikely lot of travelers. They include the young socialite Iris Henderson; Gilbert, a folk music expert; two English gentlemen, worried about arriving in England in time for a cricket match; a bickering married couple; and Miss Froy, a slightly dotty old governess, the "lady" of the title.

At the inn, Miss Froy and Iris unite to uncover the source of a horrible noise. It turns out to be Gilbert recording native folk songs and dances. He and Iris fight. Like Donat and Carroll in *The 39 Steps*, the two have a sparring relationship that masks their attraction.

There is one sinister hint of foul play to come. As Miss Froy listens dreamily to a guitarist playing below her window, a shadowy hand grabs him and pulls him away.

The next morning, the travelers prepare to board a train. Iris, soon to be married to a dull, if rich, young man, bids a sad farewell to her friends. Miss Froy takes Iris under her wing after Iris is hit by a flowerpot that falls from an

Miss Froy makes her travel arrangements.

upstairs window. On the train, the eccentric Miss Froy instructs the steward to serve her only the special brand of tea she hands him.

Exhausted from the blow to her head, Iris falls asleep. Her last sight is of a man in her train compartment performing a little magic trick for his son.

When Iris awakes, Miss Froy has vanished. The other passengers swear they never saw an old English woman. As Iris searches frantically for Miss Froy, she bumps into Gilbert. "If it isn't Old Stinker," he says, but her injury arouses his sympathy. Together they ask fellow passenger Dr. Hartz, a noted brain surgeon, to help them in their quest—but to no avail.

Miss Froy had written her name on the window while she and Iris
had tea.

At the next stop, Dr. Hartz's patient, bandaged from
head to toe, is loaded on. Iris and Gilbert watch for Miss
Froy to disembark, but they see nothing.

Other passengers also deny Miss Froy's existence, all
for their own reasons. Dr. Hartz says Iris must be hal-
lucinating because of her head injury. When another
lady mysteriously shows up—a Madame Kummer—they
all decide she must have been the lady Iris spoke of.

Iris admits defeat. At tea with Gilbert, however, she
sees the word "Froy" on the fogged-up window, where
Miss Froy had written it hours before. But Gilbert doesn't

see it. Unsure and frightened, Iris pulls the emergency brake on the train, then passes out.

When she comes to, Dr. Hartz and Gilbert try to convince her to get off with the doctor at the next station, where he will be operating on his patient. But Gilbert changes his mind when he sees in the kitchen garbage the tea label Iris mentioned as Miss Froy's special brand—proof that Miss Froy *was* on the train.

Iris and Gilbert search the baggage compartment. They discover magic act equipment, property of the magician who had been in Iris's compartment. The magician is up to no good, however; he and Gilbert struggle, and Gilbert shoves him into a trunk. But it's another magic act prop and has a false bottom. The magician escapes.

Gilbert and Iris run to the doctor for help, but his compartment is empty except for his patient and the deaf nun who attends the patient. Iris notices that the nun is wearing high heels, unusual footwear for a nun. Suddenly, it comes to Gilbert: the bandaged patient loaded on was Mme. Kummer; the patient now bandaged is poor Miss Froy. What they can't figure out, of course, is why.

Dr. Hartz walks in as they are unwrapping the bandage. He shoos them out, arranging to meet them in the dining car. When they leave, the nun exclaims to Hartz—in a London accent—"You didn't tell me she was British!" As usual in a Hitchcock movie, few people are what they seem to be. Hartz gives the nun some pills, instructing her to pass them on to the steward, who will dope up Iris and Gilbert's drinks.

In the dining car, Iris reveals their theory to Dr. Hartz. The doctor listens sympathetically, urging her to drink. He makes a toast: "May our enemies, if they exist, be unconscious of our purpose."

Iris can't tell who's who on this train.

Back in the sleeping compartment, the doctor confirms that Miss Froy is indeed the patient. More alarming, he is a member of the conspiracy. He will be "operating—unsuccessfully" on Miss Froy. He warns them that they will soon pass out, which they do.

But the nun has betrayed the doctor—out of loyalty to

her fellow Britisher—and Gilbert "awakes" immediately. He rescues the dazed Miss Froy and replaces her with Mme. Kummer. They almost get away with the switch, but the doctor discovers them while the train is still in the station. He has the police divert the train.

By the time Iris and Gilbert understand their predicament, they are holed up in hostile territory, with unfriendly police and the evil Dr. Hartz surrounding the train. Running to the dining car, they appeal to all the British passengers. It's now the Brits against the foreigners in a shoot-out.

Miss Froy reveals to Iris and Gilbert that she is a spy, entrusting Gilbert with her message in case she doesn't survive. The message is contained in the tune she heard at the Alpine chalet. Gilbert quickly learns it and Miss Froy runs off into the woods.

After more struggle, Gilbert manages to get the train running again and they chug across the border, to safety, Gilbert whistling all the way. Back in London, Iris and Gilbert say goodbye as she prepares to meet her fiancé. At the last minute, however, she jumps into a cab with Gilbert—and into his arms—and they speed toward the Foreign Office (which is sort of like the U.S. State Department).

There, the only song Gilbert can think of is the wedding march. But piano chords from the next room bring the secret tune back as they walk in and are reunited with Miss Froy.

HITCHCOCK'S TRADEMARK CAMEOS

Dame May Whitty was a famous stage actress in Britain ("Dame" is a woman's equivalent of knighthood and the title "Sir"), but Hitchcock didn't give her any special treatment. In the middle of shooting the first scene, the director interrupted her in mid-sentence, criticizing her for an awful performance. Although he wasn't completely satisfied with her performance, it wasn't as terrible as he pretended. He scolded her to get her rattled, and it worked. She played the part of the shaky old lady exactly as he wanted her to.

In this film, Hitchcock makes his trademark cameo (walk-on) appearance at the London railroad station. The director made his first film appearance by chance in his silent film *The Lodger*. One scene needed an extra person in the background, so Hitchcock volunteered. The accidental appearance turned into a superstition for Hitchcock, then his trademark and a game for the audience. Audiences were so preoccupied with finding Hitchcock in his movies that he began showing up early in a movie so that people would pay attention to the actual film, not to spotting him!

(1943)

SHADOW OF A DOUBT

b/w
pro Jack H. Skirball
sc Thornton Wilder, Alma Reville, and
  Sally Benson
st Joseph Cotten (Charlie Oakley), Teresa
  Wright (Charlie Newton)

In 1939, after the success of *The 39 Steps* and *The Lady Vanishes*, Hitchcock signed a contract with producer David O. Selznick and moved to Hollywood. Hitchcock's first American film, *Rebecca*, starring the famous British stage actor Laurence Olivier, won the Oscar for best picture. Hitchcock's next four movies did well at the box office, but *Shadow of a Doubt* is a cut above the rest.

Shadow of a Doubt sets the tone for many of his later films. Not nearly as light and breezy as his British films, this movie features a psychopathic killer lurking within a seemingly ordinary family. *Shadow of a Doubt* combines a character study with a thriller into a seamless and suspenseful whole.

The Newton family welcomes Uncle Charlie to Santa Rosa.

"The World Is a Foul Place."

In a run-down, industrial part of an East Coast city, two men are tailing Charles Oakley, a cold, angry man. To escape, Oakley heads to Santa Rosa, California, to visit his sister's family, the Newtons.

Santa Rosa is a pretty little all-American town, and the Newtons are a friendly, average American family. They greet Charles with joy, especially the restless, idealistic young Charlie, his niece and namesake. She thinks Uncle Charlie is just the person to shake things up around the quiet town. Young Charlie and Uncle Charlie share the same name, and, she believes, a special kinship. They're two of a kind and can keep no secrets from each other. She insists he stay in her room, and she sleeps in her younger sister's room.

Unlike the cold-blooded man we saw earlier, Uncle Charlie now appears as kind, jovial, and charming. The entire town admires him, and he agrees to give a speech to the local community club.

At dinner, he gives an emerald ring to young Charlie. She is surprised by the engraving on it: "To T.S." In the dining room, Charlie hums a little tune. Uncle Charlie is strangely upset by the song.

Uncle Charlie's odd behavior continues. He destroys Mr. Newton's evening paper and is angry when young Charlie declares, "You can't hide anything from me." He roughly wrests the paper from her hands.

Next he blows up at his doting sister Emma, who has invited two young men in to conduct a survey of their family. Then he behaves inappropriately at Mr. Newton's bank. When young Charlie scolds him, he just says, "The whole world's a joke to me." His charming mask is cracking as he reveals his true nature—a person who is alienated from everyone and everything, who believes in nothing.

When the two Charlies return home, Mr. Graham and Mr. Saunders, the pollsters, are there. When Saunders takes a photo of Uncle Charlie, he forces Saunders to give him the film. Young Charlie doesn't understand why her beloved uncle acts this way. But he is only one of many people who are not what they seem. That evening, on a date with Mr. Graham, Charlie realizes he's a detective. She is angry because she thinks he only asked her out to get information from her.

Still, Graham has raised enough doubts about Uncle Charlie to convince the young woman not to reveal Graham's identity. Her worst fears are confirmed when she finds the newspaper article Uncle Charlie destroyed— about "The Merry Widow Murderer," a man who romances rich widows, then strangles them. She suddenly realizes that the waltz she was humming is the Merry Widow Waltz. She also realizes that the ring Uncle Charlie gave her belonged to his latest victim.

Scared, angry, and betrayed, young Charlie now avoids Uncle Charlie, who doesn't know she's discovered his awful secret. His disguise continues to crumble, however. At dinner that night, he bursts into a tirade against widows: "Are they human or are they fat, wheezing animals?"

Uncle Charlie soon discovers that his niece is onto him. First he tries being nice, then he appeals to her as a sophisticated woman of the world. As he speaks, his hands twist a cocktail napkin as if he were wringing someone's neck. Finally, he speaks as himself, an angry, bitter man: "You're just an ordinary little girl in an ordinary little town. You live in a dream. The world is a foul place. Wake up, Charlie." She agrees to help him when he says that the truth would "kill your mother."

Charlie identifies even more with her uncle by keeping his secret for him. In return, he agrees to leave Santa Rosa. His plans change, however, when he learns that another suspect has been arrested for his crimes and the case is closed. He is very close to losing control, though. As he watches his niece out in the yard, his hands make strangling motions. Jack Graham leaves town, but returns on unofficial business—he and young Charlie have fallen in love.

Young Charlie slips on the back stairs and discovers that they were booby-trapped. Next her uncle traps her in the garage with the car running, but a neighbor comes by and foils his murder attempt. Even Emma can't help wondering about this strange series of "accidents."

That night, after Uncle Charlie gives his speech at the

The two Charlies

local club, he announces to the Newtons' guests that he
will leave Santa Rosa the next morning. Coincidentally,
Mrs. Potter, a wealthy widow, will be riding the same train.
His sister cries, and the mayor laments the departure of
such a fine citizen. Only young Charlie looks on coldly.
Her secret separates her from her happy family—she is
just as alone as Uncle Charlie.

The next morning, Uncle Charlie lures young Charlie
onto the train. He tries to throw her from the train—she
knows too much. In the struggle, she breaks free and accidentally pushes him out, into the path of an oncoming
train. She and Jack Graham are the only ones who will
ever know Uncle Charlie's secret. They sit outside the

chapel while the minister delivers a eulogy for Uncle Charlie, praising the beauty of his soul and the sweetness of his character.

With the horrible knowlege Uncle Charlie has brought her, young Charlie now sees the world as an empty place, as her uncle saw it. The happy illusion of small-town America will never be the same for her.

ON LOCATION IN SANTA ROSA

Shadow of a Doubt was filmed on location in Santa Rosa. Hitchcock and playwright Thornton Wilder, who also wrote the movie's screenplay, spent two months in Santa Rosa before shooting began. They used many of the town's citizens as extras, and Edna May Wonacott, the daughter of a local grocer, won a supporting role as Ann, Charlie's precocious younger sister.

Hitchcock even picked out the house that the Newtons would live in. Wilder thought it was too large a house for a bank teller like Mr. Newton, but when they checked with the home's owner, it turned out he made about the same amount of money as a bank teller. Unfortunately, the owner was so excited that the film crew was going to use his house that he fixed it up before shooting began. Hitchcock's crew had to make the home look a little more run-down!

STRANGERS ON A TRAIN

b/w
pro Alfred Hitchcock
sc Raymond Chandler and Czenzi Ormonde,
   from the novel by Patricia Highsmith
st Robert Walker (Bruno Anthony), Farley
   Granger (Guy Haines), Ruth Roman
   (Ann Morton)

Strangers on a Train was the first of a series of remarkable films Hitchcock made when he was at peak form. It is another story in which an innocent, weak character slowly comes to identify with the murderous desires of a stronger, evil character. Hitchcock chose a particularly charming villain in Robert Walker, who usually played nice boy-next-door types. Hitchcock's decision to cast an actor who was known as a nice guy lived up to his motto: "The more successful the villain, the more successful the picture."

"Now You've Got Me Acting Like a Criminal."

Two pairs of feet walk toward each other in a train station. They're on a collision course—on the train, one pair of feet bumps into the other as two men sit down and cross their legs. The men are Guy Haines, a tennis star, and his talkative, rather odd fellow passenger, Bruno Anthony.

Bruno knows a lot about Guy, more than Guy likes. He knows, for example, that Guy would like to divorce his unfaithful wife and marry Ann Morton, a senator's daughter. Bruno's manner is very strange. He acts almost like a boy, wearing a silly tie "because my mother gave it to me." The son of wealthy parents, he's never had to prove himself, and he feels like a failure, which he blames on his stern, unloving father.

Gradually, Bruno brings up the subject of murder. He suggests that he "swap" murders with Guy: Bruno will kill Guy's wife, Miriam, and Guy will kill Bruno's father. It's the perfect motiveless murder, since no one will know they ever met. "See? Crisscross," says Bruno, like the two crisscrossed tennis rackets on the cigarette lighter that Guy leaves on the train.

Guy makes a joke of it, but deep down the idea appeals to him. He gets off the train in the town of Metcalf, to try once again to convince his wife to give him a divorce. Miriam refuses, however. She'll thwart his plans from spite, to keep him from the woman he really loves. They argue violently in front of her coworkers at the music store, and later he tells Ann, "I could strangle her."

In the meantime, Bruno continues with his "mission," tracking Miriam down at an amusement park. Although she's accompanied by two men, she responds flirtatiously to Bruno's intense gaze. As in many Hitchcock movies, romantic and murderous impulses get mixed together.

Bruno strangles her, not in a dark alley, but on a "Magic Isle" where lovers go, with carnival music blaring in the

Bruno stalks Miriam at the amusement park.

background. The murder is seen in the distorted "fun-
house mirror" reflection of Miriam's glasses, which fall
from her face as she dies.

Bruno triumphantly presents Miriam's cracked glasses
to Guy as proof of her death. He presses Guy to keep his
end of their "bargain." Guy is horrified, but cornered—
his knowledge makes him, at the very least, an accomplice
to murder. When a police car drives by, Guy jumps behind the gate where Bruno is standing, and the shadows
of the bars fall across their faces like the bars of a prison
cell. Guy yells, "Now you've got *me* acting like a crim-
inal—you crazy fool!" Bruno bristles at the word "crazy"
but regains his composure and tries to calm Guy: "You

must be tired. I know I am—I've had a strenuous day. Now, about my father...."

Later, Ann, her father the senator, and her younger sister Barbara (played by Hitchcock's daughter Patricia) "break" the news of Miriam's murder to Guy. He is a natural suspect, and when his alibi falls through, the police place him under an around-the-clock watch.

Bruno follows Guy relentlessly, calls him at the senator's house, and sends him letters. Bruno shows up uninvited at a party the senator hosts, spouting nonsense to the guests. He entices a judge's wife into his favorite subject of conversation, how to commit the perfect murder. He asks to "borrow her neck" to demonstrate what is, according to him, the best weapon—his hands. When he sees Barbara, however, he falls into a trance, squeezing tighter and tighter on the old lady's neck until he faints.

Ann makes the connection that Barbara looks like Miriam, with the same kind of glasses. Although Ann suspects Guy, he finally explains everything to her, from the chance encounter on the train to his present dilemma.

Guy sneaks into Bruno's house to enlist the aid of Bruno's father. Bruno discovers him but lets him go. Meanwhile, Ann appeals to Bruno's mother, but she just thinks her son is up to his usual boyish pranks. Bruno tries to convince Ann that Guy is the killer, showing her Guy's lighter, which he says he found on the island where Miriam was killed. When Ann reports this to Guy, he realizes that Bruno intends to plant the lighter on the island, which will make Guy look guilty. He decides to head Bruno off and retrieve the false evidence.

But first Guy must play an important tennis match. Normally a slow, methodical player, he surprises everyone with his fierce play. (His reason, of course, is to finish

Bruno is injured when the carousel goes out of control.

the match as soon as possible, to get to Metcalf before dark.) Bruno makes his way to the Metcalf amusement park, but not before a tense moment when he accidentally drops the lighter down a storm drain.

The movie cuts back and forth between Bruno's efforts to retrieve the lighter and Guy's tennis match. Finally Guy wins and rushes to Metcalf, tailed by the cops. Seeing Guy and the police, Bruno jumps on the carousel, followed by Guy. The police accidentally shoot the carousel operator and the merry-go-round spins faster and faster.

While Guy and Bruno fight for the lighter, an old carnival hand crawls underneath the carousel platform to shut it off. (This was not a trick shot, so Hitchcock was relieved when shooting finished and the man emerged unharmed.) He arrives just in time. Bruno is just about to push Guy off the carousel.

The carousel shrieks to a halt and flies out of control. As the electrical system blows up, people and machine parts fly everywhere. A carnival worker identifies Bruno, not Guy, as the murderer. Bruno lies crushed underneath the carousel, fatally injured but still telling his false story. He dies, and the lighter falls from his lifeless hand.

Ann and Guy, with no more obstacles, marry. On a train, a clergyman looks up from his paper and asks mildly, "Aren't you Guy Haines?" Ann and Guy look at each other, laughing. Without a word, they get up and leave.

NO FREE RIDE FOR THE DIRECTOR'S DAUGHTER

Patricia Hitchcock, the director's daughter, who played Barbara, didn't get a free ride from her father. He made her go through all the steps any other actress would have to take to get the part. He interviewed her, made a screen test, and treated her coolly on the set. At home they never even discussed the movie. At the end of shooting, however, he played a little prank. He agreed to let Barbara ride on the Ferris wheel, but when she reached the top, he had the operators stop it, leaving her stranded for an hour while he went off and shot another scene in another corner of the amusement park!

46

VERTIGO

color
pro Alfred Hitchcock
sc Alec Coppel
st James Stewart (Scottie Ferguson), Kim
   Novak (Madeleine Elster/Judy Barton)

Vertigo was among Hitchcock's favorite movies, and some critics consider it his finest film, even though it wasn't a huge success when it was released. Although the movie resembles a ghost story, it is really about obsession. It reflects Hitchcock's growing interest in getting inside his characters' heads. Vertigo also brings up the familiar idea that romance and murder are linked.

"There's One Final Thing I Have to Do, Then I'll Be Free of the Past."

Even before the actual story gets rolling, Hitchcock sets the tone with a marvelous credit sequence. A close-up of a woman's face focuses on her lips and eyes. The screen turns red, and spiraling abstract patterns come whirling out of the eye's pupil, like strange images emerging from the depths of the mind. Later, other images of spirals appear in the heroine's upswept hairdo and in the winding staircase of a church bell tower.

During a rooftop chase, police detective Scottie Ferguson experiences vertigo (dizziness) and a paralyzing fear of heights at just the wrong time. As Scottie watches helplessly, another policeman falls to his death. (For this scene, Hitchcock used a very complicated shot, zooming forward with the camera lens while dollying [moving the camera on a special truck] backward. The result is a sense of dizzying motion.)

Guilt-ridden and ashamed of his weakness, Scottie quits the police force. He's soon back in the detective business, however. An old college acquaintance, Gavin Elster, fears that his wife Madeleine has been "possessed" by a dead spirit. Reluctantly, Scottie agrees to observe her at a restaurant. He is smitten and agrees to follow her.

His pursuit, unlike most Hitchcock chases, is not furious and fast paced, but slow, deliberate, and dreamlike. He follows Madeleine all over San Francisco: to a florist; to a chapel, where she visits the grave of a woman named Carlotta Valdes; to an art museum, where she looks at a portrait of Carlotta Valdes; and to a run-down hotel.

Later, Scottie and Midge, a down-to-earth career girl and Scottie's ex-fiancée, track down Valdes's story. In the late 1800s, Valdes arrived in San Francisco from a small town called San Juan Bautista, became the mistress of a wealthy tycoon, and bore his illegitimate child. He kept the child but "threw Carlotta away." The double loss of her lover and her child drove her to suicide.

Elster thinks the spirit of Carlotta has possessed his

Scottie saves Madeleine from drowning.

wife. Madeleine's increasingly strange behavior makes Elster fear that she, like Carlotta, will kill herself. While Scottie is obsessed with his fear of heights, and is slowly becoming obsessed with Madeleine, Madeleine herself appears obsessed with Carlotta.

When following Madeleine one day, Scottie rescues her after she leaps into the San Francisco Bay. He takes her to his apartment, removes her wet clothes, and puts her in his bed. When she awakes, they talk for a while—she swears she's never been to the art museum. Scottie is clearly in love. But when he returns from a phone call in the other room, Madeleine is gone.

The next day, they go for a drive into a redwood forest. In this mysterious atmosphere, she begs him not to make her reveal her secret. Driving down the coast, she tells him about a recurring nightmare in which she sees her own grave. Her mystery and vulnerability rouse his affections even more. They embrace and kiss.

Returning to the city, Scottie visits his old friend Midge. Now he also has a secret—his love for Madeleine, another man's wife.

Madeleine shows up unannounced at Scottie's. She's had the nightmare again. She describes an old Spanish mission town—Carlotta's home. Scottie takes her to the town to confront her fears and free her of them, just as he wants to face and cure his vertigo.

But his plan backfires. Madeleine, who is very agitated, professes her everlasting love for him. Then she runs up the bell tower. Scottie chases her up the stairs, but his fear of heights overcomes him and he can't reach her in time. Through a window, he watches Madeleine throw herself to her death.

Scottie is cleared of all wrongdoing, although the judge constantly refers to his "weakness" (his vertigo), which prevented him from saving Madeleine. Even though he is legally free, Scottie feels guilty. It's all too much for him—Madeleine's death, the guilt, his weakness. In a spectacular dream sequence, he imagines himself falling onto the tile roof where Madeleine's body landed. He ends up in a mental hospital, but he is soon released.

His obsession with Madeleine is not over, however. He visits the places she used to go and imagines he sees her everywhere. Finally one day, he sees a red-haired woman who reminds him of Madeleine. He follows her to her shabby hotel room and coaxes his way into her room.

Judy Barton agrees to meet Scottie for dinner.

She is Judy Barton from Salina, Kansas, a girl who's had to make her own way in the world. Reluctantly she agrees to have dinner with him.

In fact, she is "Madeleine." Judy had been Elster's mistress, and she posed as Madeleine in an elaborate plot with Elster. They used Scottie as a witness who would confirm the "suicide," when in fact Elster had murdered the real Madeleine. Elster chose Scottie because he knew his vertigo would prevent him from reaching the bell tower in time. In typical fashion, Hitchcock heightens the suspense by letting the audience in on this secret before Scottie knows.

In the course of her charade as Madeleine, Judy really did fall in love with Scottie. Even though she knows Scottie loves the delicate, mysterious Madeleine and not the person Judy really is, she agrees to date him, keeping her secret to herself. She even agrees to be made over in Madeleine's image—Scottie buys her the same suit Madeleine wore and makes Judy dye her hair and fix it

the same way as Madeleine. Only when she is completely transformed does he kiss her.

She slips up when she wears the necklace Carlotta wore in the portrait—a gift from Elster for her part in the murder plot. Scottie recognizes it and insists on a drive to the mission town. There, he refers to "one final thing I have to do, then I'll be free of the past." He needs her to "be Madeleine for a while. When it's done we'll both be free."

Judy is afraid, and with good reason. Scottie roughly forces her into the bell tower and up the stairs. He wants her to reenact the awful death scene so he'll have "a second chance," but as they climb the stairs, he tells her he has figured out the murder plot. He feels betrayed, and all because of his "weakness"—his vertigo, his love for Madeleine, his inability to save her.

For now, though, he has overcome his vertigo as he drags Judy to the top of the tower. But he realizes it's too late—he can never bring Madeleine back. In a last desperate grasp for the Madeleine who never existed, he kisses Judy passionately.

Just then she hears footsteps behind the door. It's a nun coming to investigate the commotion. Panicked, Judy backs through the window and falls to her death. Scottie has lost her again, and this time there won't be another chance. He steps to the window ledge and looks down, his own fate— the return of his vertigo, or even a descent into madness—unclear.

A DIFFICULT WORK RELATIONSHIP

Vertigo was the last of four Hitchcock movies that starred Jimmy Stewart. Along with Cary Grant, Stewart was one of Hitchcock's favorite male leads. Some people have said that Stewart's characters expressed the director's

own feelings. Whether or not this is true, their collaboration was certainly satisfying for both Hitchcock and Stewart.

On the other hand, Hitchcock and Kim Novak, who played both Madeleine and Judy, had a less-than-happy work relationship. He originally cast Vera Miles for the part. When she dropped out due to pregnancy, he grudgingly accepted Novak as a replacement—but he never warmed up to her. Years after he made *Vertigo*, Hitchcock admitted, "At least I got the chance to throw her in the water." The scene required numerous takes before Hitch was satisfied.

NORTH BY NORTHWEST

color
pro Alfred Hitchcock
sc Ernest Lehman
st Cary Grant (Roger Thornhill), Eva Marie
Saint (Eve Kendall), James Mason (Philip
Vandamm)

After the dark mood of *Vertigo*, Hitchcock returned to a more comic vein, calling on Cary Grant, another of his favorite leading men. If Jimmy Stewart was considered a stand-in for Hitchcock as he really was, Cary Grant was often said to be Hitchcock as he wanted to be: suave, handsome, a success with women. Although Grant was 54 when he made *North by Northwest*, his good looks and charm seemed ageless. In fact, he was the same age as Jessie Royce Landis, the actress who played his mother in the film!

The movie is best known for two famous scenes: when Cary Grant is chased by a crop duster; and the final scene, in which he and Eva Marie Saint flee the villains by sliding down the presidents' faces on Mount Rushmore.

One of Hollywood's most popular leading men, Cary Grant, starred in four Hitchcock movies— *Suspicion* (1941), *Notorious* (1946), *To Catch a Thief* (1955), and *North by Northwest.*

The longest of Hitchcock's films (over two hours), *North by Northwest* is reminiscent of his early British films, particularly *The 39 Steps.* Like that movie, *North by Northwest* is a spy thriller with witty dialogue, fast-paced action, an elegant blond woman, and a charming hero who is accidentally dragged into a web of international intrigue, which leads him on a journey all over the country. The plot twists in *North by Northwest* were so sudden that Cary Grant complained to Hitchcock during shooting, "I can't make head or tail of this movie!" There are similarities to many other Hitchcock plots: a false death; a fascination with strangling; and a mother-dominated main character.

Many common Hitchcock themes also show up in *North by Northwest*: a police pursuit of "the wrong man" and its companion theme of mistaken identity; characters who are not what they seem. *North by Northwest* also illustrates another one of Hitchcock's favorite scenarios—how danger and chaos can erupt in the everyday lives of ordinary people.

"That Plane's Dusting Crops Where There Ain't No Crops."

Roger Thornhill is a New York ad executive who leads an entertaining, if superficial, life, "selling people things they don't need." At a business lunch at the swanky Plaza Hotel, Thornhill is mistaken for "George Kaplan" and is hustled off by two thugs. He arrives at the estate of someone named "Lester Townsend."

Townsend thinks Thornhill's story—which is the truth—is just a trick to escape. It's hard to tell who or what Townsend is, but he's clearly up to no good. When Thornhill refuses to cooperate (since he has no idea what he's supposed to do or say), the two thugs pour bourbon down his throat, put him behind the wheel of a car, and set it off down a winding road. Thornhill miraculously survives, but not before he causes an accident and is hauled in by the police for drunk driving.

The police don't believe Thornhill's story. Not even his mother believes him—it just sounds too preposterous. Worse, when Thornhill and his mother return to the mansion to try to prove his story, the "lady of the house" pretends to be old friends with Roger, and her "husband," Mr. Townsend, is a member of the United Nations.

Roger and his mother track down Kaplan's suite at the Plaza, only to discover he was never there. The two thugs have followed Thornhill, however. He and his mother escape into a crowded elevator. The goons jump in at the last minute and Mrs. Thornhill turns to them, asking, "You gentlemen aren't *really* trying to kill my son, are you?" Everyone in the elevator bursts into laughter.

Thornhill races to the United Nations and tracks down Townsend—but it's not the same man. The man at the UN *is* the real Mr. Townsend. Before Thornhill can unravel the mystery, Townsend is killed by a knife in the back. Thornhill reaches down to pull the knife out, and a newspaper photographer snaps his photo. Roger is now a wanted man.

Kaplan, we learn, doesn't exist; he's a decoy set up by U.S. intelligence operations to throw spies like "Townsend" (whose real name is Philip Vandamm) off the right track. The head of intelligence operations plans to let Roger serve as bait to protect their real agent, even if it means that Roger is captured by the police, or worse, killed.

Hunted by the police and the spies, Roger sets off on a wild goose chase—trying to find the nonexistent Kaplan. Roger hops the train to Chicago. Fleeing the police, he bumps into an attractive blonde, Eve Kendall. She throws the police off his trail. They meet again in the dining car, exchanging romantic conversation. Eve continues to cover for him, hiding him in her upper bunk.

There's the usual confusion between murder and romance, as Roger emerges from his hiding place and Eve asks him, "How do I know you're not a murderer?"

Roger replies, "You don't. Shall I?" (Murder you, that is.)

"Please do," she answers, clearly with romance, not murder, on her mind.

Once again, we learn more than Thornhill: Eve is in cahoots with Vandamm. In Chicago, she "helps" Roger escape through the train station and arranges a meeting with Kaplan (whom the spies still believe exists) in a desolate prairie in the middle of nowhere.

Roger disembarks from a Greyhound bus into the middle of flat farmland, impatiently waiting for Kaplan. After a long wait (several minutes of complete silence on-screen), a local man comes to board the next bus. As he gets on, he remarks to Thornhill, "That's funny...that plane's dusting crops where there ain't no crops."

Alone again, Roger idly watches the plane until he figures out that it's headed straight toward him! He throws himself on the ground, narrowly escaping machine-gun fire, then tries to run for cover. There's no cover to be found, though, not even a tree. Finally, he saves himself by forcing an oil truck to a screeching halt right in the plane's path. As onlookers drive up and get out of their cars to watch the explosion, Roger makes off with one of the cars and speeds back to Chicago.

Unlike many of Hitchcock's most famous scenes, for the crop duster scene, he created suspense not by using faster and faster cuts, but by setting the scene in broad daylight and using shots of the same length. By stretching out these long periods of emptiness, he lets us know that *something* will happen. Like Roger, the audience doesn't know exactly what or when until it happens.

Roger's growing suspicions about Eve are confirmed when he sees her in Chicago. He follows her to her hotel room, then to an art auction, where she's sitting with Vandamm, his arm around her shoulder. Roger feels twice betrayed: she's set him up for murder, and on top of that she's got another boyfriend.

Roger confronts them at the auction, threatening to tell all to the police. When Vandamm's thugs block the exits, Roger makes a spectacle of himself so he'll be arrested and taken into the custody of the police. (When they finally hustle him off, he asks, "What took you so long?") They quickly release him into the hands of the intelligence officer, who asks for his help. Thornhill gives in when they dangle Eve's safety before him—she's a double agent. Thornhill, now that he knows Eve isn't in love with Vandamm, is eager to be reunited with her.

Roger, Eve, and Vandamm meet again at Mount Rushmore. In the tourist center restaurant, Eve shoots Roger (with blank bullets), trying to convince Vandamm of her loyalty. The intelligence officer arranges for Roger and Eve to meet secretly in the woods behind Mount Rushmore. He also reveals that Eve will not remain with Roger but must fly off with Vandamm. The circle of deceit is now complete: "the good guys" have tricked Roger into working for them, making a promise they know they won't keep.

Roger goes to Vandamm's secret hideout and watches as Vandamm realizes the shots were blank. Roger sneaks upstairs to warn Eve that her cover is blown, but he is trapped by the housekeeper while Vandamm drags Eve towards the getaway plane. Escaping from the housekeeper, Roger grabs Eve from Vandamm, and the two slip

and slide down the face of Mount Rushmore to escape Vandamm.

Roger and Eve hang on by their fingernails as a spy stomps on his hands. In the nick of time, the U.S. intelligence agents come over the hill. The final shot shifts from the heights of Mount Rushmore to Roger pulling Eve—now Mrs. Thornhill—to the upper bunk in a train car, as the train disappears into a tunnel.

FILMING AT MOUNT RUSHMORE

The shots of the United Nations lobby were made with an exact copy, because shooting was prohibited on the UN premises. Hitchcock managed to sneak in a shot of Grant entering the real building, however, using a hidden camera while guards were busy searching the film crew's equipment.

Hitchcock had wanted to use Mount Rushmore in a film for years. The United States government was not very cooperative in the filming, however. Government officials revoked Hitchcock's permit when they learned exactly what the director was planning, calling it "desecration" of a national monument.

The newspapers blew up the issue even more, some comparing it to "scampering on the Queen's face," which was supposed to make the Englishman Hitchcock understand the enormity of the insult. Finally, the government agreed to allow Hitchcock to have his characters slide in between the presidents' faces or below the chins.

Hitchcock, for his part, thought the whole thing was ridiculous. With his typical humor, he saw the controversy as a lost opportunity. He wanted to hang Cary Grant from Abraham Lincoln's nostril "and let him have a sneezing fit."

PSYCHO

b/w
pro Alfred Hitchcock
sc Joseph Stefano, from the novel by
   Robert Bloch
st Anthony Perkins (Norman Bates), Janet
   Leigh (Marion Crane)

Psycho is one of Hitchcock's masterpieces, and to this day it remains a hallmark in the horror genre. The movie, which won Hitchcock a best director Academy Award nomination, has often been imitated but never equaled. It caused a great stir when it was released, because Hitchcock insisted that no one be allowed to enter the theater once the movie started.

The movie shows the most explicit violence of any Hitchcock movie (though it's not very violent by today's standards). Hitchcock insisted that it was a "fun" picture, however, like going to the haunted house at the fair. Actually, the movie was so shocking that the humor came as a necessary relief to the tension.

Psycho features a psychopathic killer, like Uncle Charlie in *Shadow of a Doubt* and Bruno in *Strangers on a Train.* While Norman Bates, the killer in *Psycho,* is not as smooth and charming as these two, he is likable—likable enough that we begin to see the world through his eyes. As Bates says, "We all go a little mad from time to time."

Psycho takes the theme of mother domination to its peak. *Psycho* also deals with two themes that surface in other Hitchcock movies: voyeurism and Hitchcock's obsession with birds.

Voyeurism means spying on other people: taking pleasure from watching people who don't know they're being watched. Many film critics believe that watching movies is a form of voyeurism: we sit "hidden" in a dark room, watching people's stories unfold. Hitchcock hinted at this idea in many films, particularly *Rear Window* (1954), in which a bedridden man witnesses a murder from the back window of his apartment. In *Psycho,* he fully explores the idea.

Hitchcock also used birds as a symbol of chaos in other movies, but in *Psycho* the connection is made more clear. The movie's leading lady is named after a bird (Marion "Crane"), and the leading man stuffs birds as a hobby. He even looks something like a bird, with a thin, gawky neck and a prominent, beaklike nose. Hitchcock took the theme to its extreme in his next movie, *The Birds.*

"A Boy's Best Friend Is His Mother."

In Phoenix, Arizona, Marion Crane is having a lunchtime rendezvous with her lover, Sam Loomis, in a cheap hotel room. Marion wants to marry Sam, but he can't afford it—he has to pay alimony to his ex-wife and pay off his dead father's debts.

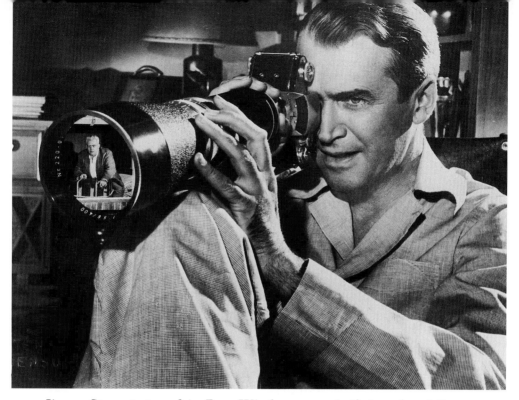

Jimmy Stewart starred in *Rear Window*, a movie that explored the theme of voyeurism.

Back at Marion's office, a slightly tipsy client, Mr. Cassidy, comes in. Marion's boss gives her $40,000 of Cassidy's money to deposit in the bank on her way home. But instead of going straight to the bank, Marion goes home. She struggles with her conscience, but she finally decides to steal the money and meet Sam in California, where he lives. This way, she thinks, they'll have enough money to get married.

On her way out of Phoenix, Marion sees her boss crossing the street. He looks at her strangely, wondering why she hasn't gone home yet. As she drives out of the city, she gets sleepy and pulls to the side of the road to sleep. When she wakes, a state trooper questions her. We feel nervous for Marion and are relieved when he lets her go.

She buys a used car with California license plates, paying with cash from her stolen money. When it gets dark outside and begins to rain harder and harder, Marion loses her way. She's relieved to find shelter from the storm in the form of a neon sign: "Bates Motel."

Norman Bates runs down from the old creepy mansion behind the motel to greet Marion, who registers under a false name. She and Norman chat. He's a little nervous, but he seems like a nice young man. Since she's the only guest, he invites her for supper to his house, where he lives with his mother. But as Marion unpacks in her room, she can hear Mrs. Bates harshly scolding her son, forbidding him to invite her up, because girls are "cheap" and "dirty."

Norman returns to the motel and asks her into his office for a sandwich. He apologizes for his mother, saying she "isn't quite herself today." Norman's office is full of stuffed birds, since his hobby is "stuffing things." He explains that he has no friends, because "a boy's best friend is his mother."

Norman talks about how people are in their own private traps. When Marion suggests that sometimes we set our own traps, Norman pathetically replies, "I was born into mine." He recoils, however, at Marion's suggestion that he put his mother into a nursing home. "My mother's as harmless as one of these stuffed birds," he says.

Marion returns to her room and decides to free herself from her own trap and return the money. Before retiring, she decides to take a shower. Meanwhile, Norman spies on her through a hole in his office wall—and we spy along with him. We start to understand Norman a little more, seeing Marion from Norman's viewpoint.

Marion steps into the shower. The sound of running

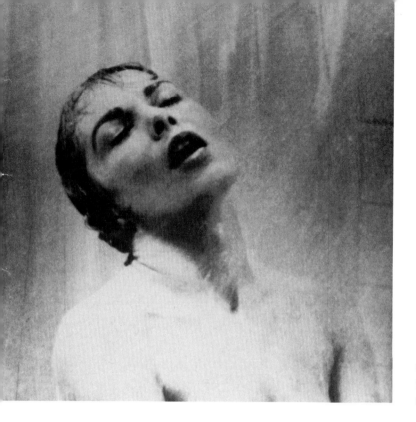

One of the most famous moments in American cinema....

water drowns out all other noise. Suddenly, an old woman enters the bathroom, whips aside the shower curtain, and starts brutally stabbing Marion, while horrible shrieking music plays in the background. We see her face close-up, screaming, and the knife plunging down, although only one shot shows the knife actually touching her flesh. She claws at the shower stall and finally slips to the floor, with one eye still open, as blood circles down the drain.

When Norman discovers what his mother has done, he cleans up the mess, loads Marion's body and her things (including the money, which he doesn't know about) into her car, and sinks it in the swamp behind the motel. Since the heroine has been murdered before the movie is even half over (a very unusual plot turn for any movie), the only person left for us to identify with is Norman. When he hides the evidence of murder, we feel relieved, just as we were relieved when Marion escaped the police officer.

Disturbed by her disappearance, Sam and Lila, Marion's sister, hire a private detective to find her. Arbogast, the detective, retraces Marion's journey to the Bates Motel and questions Norman. Norman claims he doesn't remember her, and he refuses to let Arbogast into the house, saying his mother is not well. After Arbogast calls Lila with his findings, he sneaks back to the house. As he climbs the stairs, the old lady stabs him to death.

With Arbogast gone, Sam returns to the Bates Motel. He finds nothing. He and Lila turn to the local sheriff; when they mention Mrs. Bates, he says she's been dead for years—Norman found her and her lover dead in bed. Meanwhile, Norman is getting nervous and carries his invalid mother down to the root cellar.

Sam and Lila resolve to continue the search. They register at the Bates Motel, unaware that Norman was watching when Sam searched for Arbogast. Sam decoys Norman in conversation while Lila goes up to the house. She looks in Mrs. Bates's room and notices that a body has recently been in the bed. Then she heads up to Norman's attic room, which looks more like a boy's room than a grown man's.

When Marion sees Norman coming, she descends to the cellar. She opens the cellar door, and there, in the light of a bare lightbulb swinging back and forth, she finally discovers Mrs. Bates—a mummified corpse sitting in a rocking chair! Still, the homicidal old lady comes up behind her, knife raised. Sam arrives in the nick of time, and as he wrestles with the old woman, her wig falls off to reveal Norman, dressed as his mother, about to commit another murder.

At the end, a psychiatrist explains the situation: Trapped by a selfish, domineering mother, Norman finally killed her and her lover. But he couldn't stand the guilt of killing his own mother, so he kept her corpse "alive." He gradually became a split personality. The "good" Norman could deny his murderous side, since it was "Mother" doing those horrible things. Despite this explanation, the pyschiatrist's manner isn't quite trustworthy, so we don't know whether to believe him.

As for Norman, he sits in a room in solitary confinement, wrapped in a blanket and lost in his own psychotic world. We hear his thoughts in his mother's voice. She thinks about how sad it is to have to condemn her own son. But she knows she "had" to. She's not a bad person—she wouldn't even hurt a fly.

The final shot shows Marion's car being dredged up from the swamp.

AFRAID TO TAKE A SHOWER?

Nothing like *Psycho* had ever appeared on movie screens before. The shower scene especially had such a tremendous effect that some people swore they were afraid to step into the shower for years afterward. According to Hitchcock, one man finally wrote to him in desperation, asking for advice about his wife, who was so terrified she refused to shower or bathe. Hitchcock replied, "Sir, have you considered sending your wife to be dry-cleaned?"

Tippi Hedren had to get used to birds—near her, around her, and on her—during the making of *The Birds*.

THE BIRDS

(1963)

color
pro Alfred Hitchcock
sc Evan Hunter, from the short story by
   Daphne du Maurier
st Tippi Hedren (Melanie Daniels), Rod
   Taylor (Mitch Brenner), Jessica Tandy
   (Mrs. Brenner), Suzanne Pleshette
   (Annie Hayworth)

About three years passed between the time *Psycho* came out and the release of *The Birds,* the longest period Hitchcock had spent without making a movie. Although Hitchcock made five more movies after *The Birds,* they were—by Hitchcock standards—not of the same quality as his previous films.

All of Hitchcock's movies show how ordinary lives can suddenly be turned upside down. In *The Birds,* the director's fascination with birds as a symbol of chaos reaches its full measure. In *Psycho,* Norman and birds were compressed into one character, and even though we identified with him, he was just one person, not the whole world. In *The Birds,* chaos is everywhere—we can't escape it.

The movie also mixes horror and science fiction. Although birds are normally harmless creatures—Hitchcock was careful not to use birds of prey—the birds in this movie become like alien invaders. Some people, especially in the late 1960s when the ecology movement was beginning, felt that the movie foretold the consequences of human mistreatment of the environment: nature would eventually rise up and take revenge.

Although terrifying, *The Birds* was not as big a success as *Psycho* and was often criticized for its ending, which did not wrap up the story neatly.

"Can I Take My Lovebirds Along?"

Melanie Daniels, a rich young woman from San Francisco, meets Mitch Brenner in a pet store. Mitch, a handsome, self-assured lawyer, is buying a pair of lovebirds for his much younger sister, Cathy. He helps capture a canary that has gotten loose in the store. In this scene, the importance of birds is already clear, but they will soon change from cute little pets to something much more dangerous.

Mitch is attracted to Melanie (who poses as a store clerk) and the two trade witty remarks. Impulsively, Melanie agrees to deliver the lovebirds to Mitch's weekend home in the northern California town of Bodega Bay. Mitch lives there with Cathy and his widowed mother, Lydia.

The Brenners live across the bay from the main street of town. When Melanie boats back from Mitch's place, a seagull swoops down out of the blue and scratches her. She returns to Mitch's house for supper and decides to attend Cathy's birthday party the next day.

Although Cathy and Mitch like Melanie, their mother is cold and unfriendly. When Melanie spends the night at a neighbor's house, she learns why. Annie Hayworth,

At the beginning of the movie, Melanie is cool and well groomed. By the end, she is terrified and bedraggled.

the local schoolteacher, was once romantically involved with Mitch, although he's no longer interested. Annie says that Mitch could never be interested in another woman for very long because of Lydia, his mother.

But Annie likes Lydia, and now that they're no longer competing for Mitch's affection, Lydia likes Annie, too. Lydia is a nice lady, but she is so afraid of being left alone that she has become jealous and possessive.

At Cathy's birthday party, birds start attacking the children. That evening, a flock of sparrows flies down the Brenners' chimney, and Mitch lights a fire to shoo them out. The sparrows don't hurt the Brenners or Melanie, but they cause a lot of damage. Lydia is upset and cracks her tea set.

The next day, Lydia goes to a neighboring farmer's house. There are broken teacups in this house, too. We realize with growing dread that something awful must have

happened here, too. Sure enough, Lydia finds the farmer dead, his eyes pecked out.

As the children leave school that day, a flock of crows gathers ominously, at first just a few of them sitting on the phone wires, then, gradually, a mass of them perched on every rung of the jungle gym. Melanie and Annie herd the kids to safety, but Annie dies trying to protect them.

Melanie and the children take shelter in the town cafe, where various town characters try to explain what the birds mean. A drunk says the odd attacks signal the end of the world; a bookish ornithologist (a scientist who studies birds) dismisses the whole thing; some townspeople accuse Melanie of witchcraft; and one man thinks the town should just bring in the army and blast the birds.

None of these explanations work, though—there really is no explanation. And the danger soon returns. The birds swoop down on the main street, attacking a gas station attendant and causing him to spill gasoline all over. The man who wanted to blast the birds away drops his cigarette butt. The gasoline ignites, and the man dies in the explosion.

Melanie hides in a phone booth, which the birds peck to pieces. The radio reports that huge flocks of birds have been seen heading for Santa Rosa. The Brenners and Melanie barricade themselves into their house as the birds hurl themselves against the doors and windows.

They survive the attack, but Melanie goes to investigate sounds in the attic. To her horror, it's full of birds, and they fly at her ferociously. Mitch rescues her, and the Brenners realize they must get Melanie to a hospital. Besides, they know it is hopeless to hold out any longer against the birds. As the birds pause briefly in their attacks, the family manages to drive away. As they leave, we see the flocks and flocks of birds perched silently—waiting.

THE BIRDS ARE TIRED!

As with most of Hitchcock's movies, he tried to make *The Birds* as realistic as possible. Much of the shooting was done on location, in Bodega Bay, and the sets were based on real buildings and houses. Likewise, costumes were based on the clothing of the real townspeople. Even the scene in which the farmer has his eyes pecked out was inspired by a local newspaper article about crows attacking lambs.

Of course, the movie posed huge challenges. Hitchcock used almost 400 trick shots out of a total 1,360 shots in the movie. (An average 90-minute movie uses about 600 shots; the average Hitchcock movie used about 500.) To create the effect of attacking birds, Hitchcock used a combination of animation, mechanical birds, composite shots (several shots combined into one), and trained birds. No real birds were used in the scenes with children.

It was a complicated job to film the bird attacks.

Mechanical birds were supposed to be used for the attic scene at the movie's end, but at the last minute Hitchcock used real birds. As with the shower scene in *Psycho*, there was a week of filming for about two minutes of on-screen time. Actress Tippi Hedren called it "the worst week of her life." Birds were tied to her with rubber bands to keep them from flying away. She had to endure birds flying at her, though none attacked her. She did get hurt, however, when a gull perched on her eyelid, almost putting her eye out. The actress was so upset that filming stopped for a week while she regained her physical health and her composure.

The birds, on the other hand, fared much better. Humane Society officials were on hand to make sure the animals were treated properly. According to Hedren, "Promptly at five o'clock, someone from the society would announce, 'Quitting time! The birds are tired.'"

Epilogue

Hitchcock made five more movies after *The Birds.* His last movie, *Family Plot,* came out in 1976. He was working on another film when he died at the age of 80.

In his later years, the director finally received the recognition he deserved from the film community, and he was knighted by Queen Elizabeth a few months before he died. His films have spawned a host of imitators. One director, Brian De Palma, has made many thrillers using plots, themes, and even camera angles and shots deliberately borrowed from Hitchcock. Mel Brooks, a comedian, made a movie called *High Anxiety* that spoofed Hitchcock, especially *Vertigo.* Other directors have been influenced by Hitchcock without even realizing it.

Perhaps Hitchcock's greatest achievement was to turn a popular form of entertainment, the suspense movie, into an art. He explored the hidden fears that we all share and still made thrilling films for everyone to enjoy.

For Further Reading

Haley, Michael. *The Alfred Hitchcock Album.* Englewood Cliffs, NJ: Prentice-Hall, Inc. 1981.

Perry, George. *Hitchcock.* New York: Doubleday, 1975.

Phillips, Gene D. *Alfred Hitchcock.* Boston: Twayne Publishers, 1984.

Sinyard, Neil. *The Films of Alfred Hitchcock.* New York: Gallery Books, 1986.

Spoto, Donald. *The Art of Alfred Hitchcock: Fifty Years of His Motion Pictures.* Garden City, NY: Doubleday & Co., 1979.

Taylor, John Russell. *Hitch: The Life and Times of Alfred Hitchcock.* New York: Pantheon Books, 1978.

Truffaut, François. *Hitchcock.* Rev. ed. with Helen G. Scott. New York: Simon and Schuster, 1983.

Index